Absolute

Wrestling Madness

John Eleuthère Du Pont and the Foxcatcher Farm Murder

ABSOLUTE CRIME

By Tim Huddleston

Absolute Crime Books
www.absolutecrime.com

© 2013. All Rights Reserved.

Cover Image © mtkang - Fotolia.com

Table of Contents

About Us

Absolute Crime publishes only the best true crime literature. Our focus is on the crimes that you've probably never heard of, but you are fascinated to read more about. With each engaging and gripping story, we try to let readers relive moments in history that some people have tried to forget.

Remember, our books are not meant for the faint at heart. We don't hold back — if a crime is bloody, we let the words splatter across the page so you can experience the crime in the most horrifying way!

If you enjoy this book, please visit our homepage to see other books we offer; if you have any feedback, we'd love to hear from you!

Prologue

Dave Schultz was in the driveway of his home on Foxcatcher Farm, putting a new radio in his Toyota Tercel, when he saw the silver Town Car heading towards him. John du Pont, the owner of the 800-acre estate where Dave lived and trained, was behind the wheel, and it looked like he had Pat Goodale in there with him. Goodale was John's security consultant, and no one on the farm liked it much when he was around. He always seemed to bring out the worst in John, and lately, John had been pretty bad on his own. Especially since Dave had made it known that after the Olympics, he was leaving Foxcatcher for good.

The Atlanta games would be Dave's last shot at another medal. He had won gold in freestyle wrestling back in 1984, but in '88 and '92, he hadn't even qualified for the team. But now, at the ripe old age of 36, he was primed for a comeback. He had placed fifth at the World Championship last summer and was currently ranked number one in the 163-pound weight class. He was stronger and faster than he'd been in years. This time, he wasn't just going to make the team, he was going to bring home another gold. It would be the perfect bookend to his competitive career, and in a lot of ways, he had John to thank for that.

John du Pont was amateur wrestling's greatest supporter and had been for the last decade. He had donated millions to the U.S. Wrestling Federation, built a state-of-the-art facility on his own property and recruited the biggest and the best names in the sport to train and coach there. It was the most elite wrestling club in the country, maybe in the world, and there was a very good possibility that the entire 1996 U.S. Olympic wrestling team was going to be made up exclusively of wrestlers from du Pont's Team Foxcatcher.

John's athletes were the children he never had, and he made sure they were well taken care of. He wanted them focused on training to be the best and not worrying about how they were going to pay their bills, so he gave them all generous monthly stipends, and in Dave's case, even a house on the estate grounds where he and his family lived rent-free. All he really wanted in return was friendship, which Dave had given willingly and gladly. But after the games, it would be time to move on. That's why he was going to accept the coaching gig Stanford had offered him.

John hadn't taken the news very well. In fact, he'd been acting like a petulant child about the whole damn thing. He refused to come over for Thanksgiving dinner and even un-invited Dave and his family to the Christmas party he held up at the mansion every year. The way John had been acting, Dave didn't expect his year-end bonus check, but sure enough, it had arrived same as always. Dave shouldn't have been surprised, though. John often let his money do his talking for him, and the check was his way of begging Dave to stay. It could be very persuasive, too.

But no, Dave's mind was made up. He had to get away from this place.

John's behavior had been getting worse, and some people were worried. Dave wasn't one of them, though. Even with all the tension right now between the two of them, when Dan Chaid, Kenny Monday and all those other wrestlers went to the federation and asked them to cut their ties to du Pont, Dave was the one who had come to his defense. But the Olympics were only seven short months away. When the games were over, Dave would be gone and John would be on his own.

Dave didn't know why John was paying him a visit on that cold, grey afternoon. But then again, you never really knew what to expect with John, anyway. It didn't matter. No matter what kind of mood he was in, Dave knew how to handle him. So, when John pulled his Lincoln into the driveway and rolled down the window, Dave approached him with a wave and a grin.

"Hey, coach," he said.

John stuck his arm outside the window. In his hand was a .44 revolver.

"You got a problem with me?" John said.

Without waiting for an answer, John pulled the trigger. Dave's elbow exploded and he screamed in surprise and agony.

"John, what are you doing?" Goodale shouted from the seat next to him as John fired another round, this one into Dave's chest. Dave stopped screaming and fell face-first into the snow. That was when John started screaming.

Dave's wife, Nancy, appeared at the front door of the house just in time to see John fire a third shot into Dave's back. John saw her on the porch and lifted the gun on her. Goodale, who was armed with two weapons, finally drew one. John wheeled on him and their barrels met.

Nancy rushed back into the house and called 911. She got through to the Newtown Square police immediately, but the dispatcher didn't seem to believe her. Was this some kind of a joke? Why would John du Pont shoot her husband?

"He's insane!" she cried.

Outside, Goodale had managed to open the car door and put one foot on the ground while he and John stared into each other's eyes over the barrels of their guns. Finally, something changed in John's cold stare. Without a word, he lowered his gun, tossed it into the back seat, put the car in reverse and backed out of the driveway. Goodale managed to get the rest of the way out of the car without injuring himself, then watched as John sped off towards the mansion.

Nancy rushed out of the house to her husband's side and took him in her arms. He was still alive, but only barely. No one could survive wounds like these, not even Dave, the strongest man she knew, the strongest man on the planet. No, Dave was going to die and he was going to die right there in front of her. She had to be strong for him, as he had been strong for her so many times in the past. "Tough as nails, Schultzie," he always said whenever the going got rough. She tried her best.

She told him she loved him and watched him exhale one last time. Nancy heard a gurgling sound — horrible in its finality — from somewhere deep inside him, and then, lying there in the embrace of his wife of fourteen years and mother of his two children, the light went out in Dave Schultz's eyes.

In the days, weeks and months that followed, the world responded in shock and horror. A member of one of the country's wealthiest and most prominent families had murdered his best friend, an Olympic gold medalist, for no apparent reason. Everything about it seemed bizarre and disconnected, but many of those who knew Dave Schultz and John du Pont were less than surprised. No one would say it better than Team Foxcatcher's Kurt Angle, a wrestler who was trained by Schultz himself.

"People saw it coming," he said. "No one did a damn thing about it."

Chapter 1: The Family Fortune

John E. du Pont was the great-great grandson of Eleuthère Irénée du Pont, a French immigrant who first arrived on American soil on January 1st, 1800. He and his family were forced to flee France after betting on the wrong horse during the French Revolution; their support of King Louis XVI and Marie Antoinette resulted in the destruction of their home by an angry mob and very nearly cost du Pont's father his head. No longer welcome in their home country, they set sail for the United States, hoping to start a model community for French exiles like themselves.

It wasn't long before du Pont took notice of the poor quality of American-made gunpowder, and that presented him with a golden opportunity. With his background in chemistry and his overseas connections at France's royal powder works, he could manufacture a much better product at a fraction of the cost. So in 1802, on the banks of the Brandywine Creek in Delaware, he opened *E.I. du Pont de Nemours and Company*, a gunpowder mill that would grow into one of the most successful and enduring businesses in American history.

When you're in the gunpowder business, bad times are good times. The War of 1812 made the mill very profitable and by the time of the Civil War, *Du Pont* had become the Union Army's chief supplier of gunpowder and explosives. By the turn of the twentieth century, the company began to diversify into other areas, most notably the development of polymers. *Du Pont* created the first synthetic rubber, they created nylon and polyester, Kevlar, Teflon and Lycra spandex. The list goes on and on. Today, it would be difficult to go anywhere or do anything without encountering something first given to us by *Du Pont.* In other words, E.I. du Pont's descendents were among the filthiest of the filthy rich. For generations, the du Ponts only married their own cousins in an attempt to keep their wealth completely in the family, although by the end of the 19th century, that practice had started to decline. Also in decline at that time was the family's direct involvement in the company's affairs.

William du Pont, Jr.'s only real connection to the business, was enjoying the wealth it generated. He grew up at Montpelier, president James Madison's historic home in Virginia, and was educated in the best private schools. In spite of his polished upbringing however, his reluctance to bathe or change his clothes on a regular basis earned him the nickname "Dirty Willie." He was also loud and brash and more than a little odd, but that was okay for men of great wealth. It made him memorable.

Dirty Willie du Pont married Jean Liseter Austin on January 1st, 1919, the anniversary of William's great grandfather's arrival in America, and it was "The Wedding of the Century." Jean was the daughter of an executive at Baldwin Locomotive Works, a railway company that was enjoying its heyday, and her marriage into the du Pont family was a union of enough wealth to create an empire. As a wedding gift, Jean's father gave the couple 600 acres of land in Newtown Square, Pennsylvania as a wedding gift. Not to be outdone, William du Pont, Sr. built Liseter Hall on the land. It was an exact replica of the Montpelier mansion, where his son had grown up. He would feel right at home.

Jean and Dirty Willie du Pont spent most of their time and money devoted to their common love of horses. They expanded their property and developed one of the most extravagant horse farms the world had ever seen. They built barns and training tracks all over the estate grounds, including the United States' first indoor galloping track. The couple didn't rest until their facilities had become the premier place for breeding and training of race, show and hunting horses.

The way they saw it, if you were going to build something, you built the best.

Chapter 2: Mama's Boy

John Eleuthère du Pont was born on November 22, 1938, the youngest of Jean and Dirty Willie's four children. When John was two years old, his parents went through an ugly divorce and his father moved out of Liseter Hall, eventually remarrying and passing his name onto his third son, John's half-brother. The first thing Jean did after the split was give the farm a new look, painting all the buildings white with green trim, making the place her own. It wasn't long after that when John's older brother and sisters grew up and moved out, leaving Jean and young John alone on the estate with their animals and their army of servants.

Jean du Pont was a fiercely independent woman, and she took great pride in self-sufficiency. Almost all the dairy, meat and vegetables they used at the estate came from their own farm. And she wasn't content to sit back and trust her employees to run things, either — she insisted on taking an active part in the estate's day-to-day operations. Each and every morning she got up with the sun, walked down to the stables and inspected all the animals, starting with her beloved Welsh ponies. Dirty Willy had always been partial to the racing Thoroughbreds, but Jean really loved the show animals, especially the ponies and the beagles.

She worked tirelessly every day, and she made John earn his keep, too. When he wasn't helping out with chores, he sold apple cider from a stand by the highway under the watchful eye of Mr. Cherry, a farmhand who was the closest thing John had to a male role model as a boy. Mr. Cherry was responsible for watching John whenever Jean couldn't do it herself. John cared for him deeply, but Mr. Cherry was far from a father figure—John knew he had no real authority over him. In addition to instilling her work ethic in her son, Jean had also made sure he was fully aware of his place on the food chain, and that place was at the very top. Mr. Cherry was one of their servants, and John could never truly respect him. How could he respect someone who wasn't even allowed to speak unless spoken to?

Jean also made sure that John was appropriately wary of outsiders. With servants, there was nothing to fear—their allegiance and loyalty was bought and paid for. They depended on the du Ponts to feed their own families, and they would never risk jeopardizing their jobs. But you never knew with outsiders. Strangers could be dangerous, and they were not welcome on Liseter Farm. If a hiker or rider made the mistake of wandering onto the property, he was promptly told to leave, often at gunpoint, and sometimes at the order of John himself.

The only equals John had were his own family, and he saw them rarely, only when he and his mother attended the societal functions that were required of people of their stature. The rest of the time, they only had each other, and John's mother became his best and only friend. Jean taught John about farming and tending to livestock. She taught him how to ride a horse and shoot a gun. They hunted foxes together and spent long hours walking the estate grounds. Most nights, Jean would tell John a bedtime story based on the images woven into Liseter Hall's rugs or painted on the china. It was a youth filled with privilege, hard work and love, but also loneliness.

John grew into a strange and awkward-looking teenager with bad posture, yellow teeth, a big nose and almost a complete lack of chin. He attended school at Haverford, an all-boys prep academy where Pennsylvania's privileged sons were educated, and was known for being a terrible student and a worse athlete. He tried both swimming and wrestling, but had no aptitude for either. He didn't seem to fit in anywhere. Even at a place like Haverford, among the children of society's elite, John's wealth still set him apart and made him an outcast. He had never needed acceptance before—he was used to people conforming to his wants and needs. Getting people to like him and taking an interest in their lives were foreign concepts to him. Consequently, he was terrible at making friends and never dated.

But none of that really mattered. He was John du Pont. He didn't need an education or the acceptance of his peers. He had his fortune. His classmates seemed to be aware of that, too and at the end of John's senior year, he was voted both "Laziest" and "Most Likely to Succeed."

In 1957, John threw his Haverford class a huge graduation party at Liseter Hall. He would have to attend summer school to earn enough credits to claim his own diploma, but that didn't stop him from throwing the biggest bash anyone in his class had ever seen. No one could resist the opportunity to get a glimpse of the opulent estate grounds, so in spite of his lack of popularity, the party was a raging success and for once, John was the center of attention. That night was probably the greatest night he had ever had in his life, and he learned a valuable lesson.

Friendship and acceptance were things that could be bought.

Chapter 3: Renaissance Man

In the fall of 1957, John enrolled at the University of Pennsylvania after being denied admission to Cornell, the safety school of the Ivy League. He didn't take to the college environment any better than he did high school, and he spent most of his freshman year drifting aimlessly, looking for purpose and finding none. An upperclassman he knew from Haverford tried to take him under his wing and even managed to talk him into pledging a fraternity, but John still wasn't comfortable there. Before even finishing his freshman year, he withdrew from the university.

Unsure what else to do with his life, John turned to his collection. John came by his hobby of collecting honestly. His father collected Thoroughbred racehorses, his mother collected show dogs and ponies, and John collected seashells, stuffed birds and bird eggs. It was no ordinary collection, either. It was a collection so large that it would take a museum to house the entire thing. So he founded one.

When the Delaware Museum of Natural History would open its doors fifteen years later, John would make sure it was the best of its kind. So after leaving college, he traveled extensively, gathering specimens from all over the world. His father funded these expeditions, perhaps in an attempt to compensate for his virtually non-existent involvement in John's childhood, and he didn't let his son go it alone. He hired the best guide he could find, renowned shell and mollusk expert, R. Tucker Abbott. It was Abbott who found and identified most of the specimens that were gathered on these trips, even if it was John who would later take credit for them.

After a few years of traveling the world, John went back to college to finish his undergraduate studies at the University of Miami, and it was there that he embarked on his first athletic obsession.

In spite of not having excelled at the sport at Haverford, John joined the University of Miami's swim team. He was welcomed with open arms, although his major contributions to the organization came more from his checkbook than any athletic ability. He didn't delude himself over that fact, either. People who knew him at the time seemed to think that he didn't feel very good about himself. The more time he spent away from Liseter Farm, the more he was learning that the only thing he had going for him was his wealth. He would have traded every cent of it for a shot at athletic glory, too. He dreamed of competing in the Olympics and bringing home the gold for the U.S.A., but knew he didn't have enough talent.

Maybe, though, he had enough money.

In 1963, John left college once again and headed off to sunny California. With the handing over of another massive check, he found himself at the elite Santa Clara Swim Club, training with some of the nation's best swimmers who were preparing for the 1964 Olympics.

While the recipients of his money were happy to have him there, the other athletes were not. Santa Clara swimmers were expected to be the best of the best, and John was nowhere close to that level. His teammates had trained hard their entire lives to get where they were. Who the hell was he to buy his way on?

But John endured. He was used to people not liking him. He was used to them resenting his money. But he also believed in surrounding himself with the best. Maybe if he hung around them enough, if he watched and learned, if he was coached by the same coaches and performed the same workouts they did, maybe, eventually, he could become as good as they were. So no matter how much his teammates ignored him or how much they ridiculed him for his inability to keep up, John worked out as hard as he could every morning and every afternoon. He did everything the other swimmers did, he just did it slower. Eventually, the work ethic his mother had driven into him ended up winning John the respect of the Santa Clara swimmers. They finally accepted him, even if it was as more of a mascot than a teammate.

As the Olympics approached, John's new his friends sat him down and forced him to accept a hard truth—he was never going to make it to the games as a swimmer. It didn't matter how hard he trained, it wasn't going to happen. He just didn't have what it took. John knew they were right, but it devastated him. He had gotten his heart set on Olympic glory, so the team banded together to find a sport where John would be able to realistically compete. And what they settled on was the pentathlon.

*   *   *

The modern pentathlon is an event that combines horseback riding, shooting, fencing, swimming and running. It was almost as if it were custom-made for John du Pont. John had grown up riding some of the finest horses in the world on Liseter Farm, and since the family fortune was built on firearms, he had been shooting guns all his life, too. And maybe he wasn't a strong enough swimmer to compete at Santa Clara, but he was more than competent by pentathlete standards. To become a runner, he would need a little training, but he was certainly in good enough shape. The only thing that was totally foreign to him was fencing, and that was more about technique than athletic prowess. It was something he could learn. But the main advantage John had, the main reason the pentathlon was so perfect for him was that it was very expensive. There were few people in the world that could afford to train to proficiency in all five of the disciplines, but John would have no problem with that. No, if there was one thing John was good at, it was spending money.

With a new mission in life, he left California and returned to the estate. There, he carved out running trails all over the property, trained daily at riding and shooting, kept up his swimming by using the pool at nearby Villanova University, and hired the best fencing instructor money could buy.

In 1965, after finally earning his undergraduate degree, John traveled to Australia where he competed in and won the Australian National Pentathlon Championship. It was the first time he had ever won anything and he was filled with a sense of accomplishment and validation. He felt as if things were finally happening for him. He was an international champion. His dreams were coming true.

The rest of the sports community didn't seem to share his enthusiasm, however. There was virtually no interest in the pentathlon in Australia during the 60's, and it was widely believed that almost any American with the financial means and the most basic skill level could have traveled there and won the competition.

Score another point for the checkbook.

On the last day of 1965, one day short of the anniversary of John's great-great grandfather's arrival in America, William du Pont, Jr. died. Estranged from his father for most of his life, the most significant effect his death likely had on John was that with it came the first installment of his personal wealth to the tune of $80 million. John used some of the money to improve the training facilities on the estate grounds, most notably building an indoor pool, complete with a wall of mosaics depicting an idealized version of John himself, competing in each of the pentathlon's five disciplines.

In 1967, he hosted the National Pentathlon Championship on the course he had built with his own money and trained on every day. It was the first true test of where he fit in to the sport and he had home field advantage. He entered the competition, determined to silence the doubters who had discounted his victory in Australia. He finished in 14th place.

It was a difficult blow, but John didn't let it get him down. He redoubled his efforts in preparation of the 1968 Olympic trials. When the time came, John was one of twenty-two competitors vying for three available spots on the team. He placed 21st.

His athletic hopes dashed, John turned his attention back towards academia. He enrolled at Villanova to pursue a doctorate in natural history and renewed his focus on his museum. Now that he had wealth of his own, the time was right to begin construction. He convinced one of his uncles to donate a plot of land in the Brandywine Valley, not too far from the gunpowder mill that set his family on the path to fortune over a hundred sixty years prior. John again enlisted the help of R. Tucker Abbott, the shell and mollusk expert he traveled the world with after high school, hiring him to design and help run the museum.

Meanwhile, John did more traveling, going to the Philippines and the South Pacific where he discovered (or at least took credit for discovering) over two-dozen species of birds. He fashioned himself into an expert in the field, co-authoring a number of ornithology books that he published himself in the early 70's.

When the Delaware Museum of Natural History finally opened its doors to the public in 1972, John was very proud of what he had achieved. The entire world could now see his private collection of 66,000 birds and two million seashells. It was a world-class museum and it ensured that John would leave a legacy behind when he died. It seemed like he had finally found his place in life as a scientist and philanthropist.

But it wasn't enough.

Chapter 4: First Cracks

Up until his mid-thirties, John's behavior could be described as odd, but essentially harmless. He was nothing more than an eccentric millionaire pumping his money into his hobbies in an effort to find a sense of self-worth. But that started to change in 1974 with the kidnapping of Patty Hearst.

Patty Hearst, the granddaughter of billionaire newspaper magnate William Randolph Hearst, was abducted by an extreme group of left-wing revolutionaries called the Symbionese Liberation Army and brainwashed into joining their cause. John found the whole affair deeply disturbing. He was also the descendant of a wealthy American businessman and heir to a vast fortune. If they wanted Patty Hearst, it stood to reason that they would want him, too. And most importantly, they had gotten to her, which meant they could get to him.

He finally understood why his mother had taught him the necessity of isolation. He had spent so much of his youth traveling, but those days were over. Now that he was living full-time on the estate, he would need to keep the grounds, his mother and himself as safe as possible. It wasn't enough to drive outsiders away, as his mother had done. They had to be kept on the outside. To that end, John had the estate grounds sealed off with walls and fences. The only way inside was through a security gate that required a card key to open it.

But what if someone managed to get past the fence? Or worse, what if they were already on the grounds, hiding somewhere — maybe in the woods, waiting to pounce on him the next time he went for a jog? He needed round-the-clock personal protection, but whom could he trust? He ended up buying himself two trained German Shepherds that followed him everywhere. People might betray you, but dogs were always loyal.

Because of his growing suspicious nature, John decided it was time to start taking a more active interest in the management of his personal wealth. He needed to make sure that his fortune wasn't being embezzled away from him or used to fund causes he didn't agree with. He got a pilot's license specifically so that he could fly his helicopter to New York every day to meet personally with his financial advisors. He didn't fly alone, though — he always brought his dogs with him for protection.

Taking control of his money allowed for John to spend it exactly how he wanted to, and one of his greatest beneficiaries was the United States pentathlon team. In fact, in 1976, the depth of his generosity led to him achieving his lifelong dream of making it to the Olympics. But not as an athlete. He had donated so much money to the team that when he said he wanted to be the team manager, no one could tell him no. John had bought his way into things before, but now, he was learning how to attach strings to his funding. To set conditions. So he was given what he wanted — an Olympic sweat suit and a spot in the team photograph.

After the games, John began more or less confining himself to the grounds of Liseter Hall. He even stopped keeping up appearances at the social functions that his mother had always insisted were required of him. Now that he was closing in on forty, it seemed like it had become Jean's mission in life to marry him off. Every time he left the estate, people pushed their daughters on him, and he had grown to resent it. He had never needed the company of a woman before and he didn't need it now. It was easier just to stay home and avoid everyone altogether. Of course, that didn't always work, either, not with his mother constantly in his ear. When he couldn't stand to listen to her anymore, he'd go for a run in the woods with his dogs, or better yet, go for a long swim in the pool. No one could bother him when he was underwater. That's the only time he was truly alone.

His need for solitude caused friction with the people in his life, Tucker Abbott in particular. When it came to the museum and how it was run, it seemed as if they couldn't agree on anything, especially how much credit Abbott deserved. John settled the dispute by firing him and even went so far as to close down the museum's mollusk department. Abbott sued for breach of contract, and when the matter was settled out of court, John learned another valuable lesson about his wealth. It couldn't just be used to buy him the things he wanted, it could be used to make his problems go away.

By the late 70's, John's fears over his safety had become very profound. He decided that he needed more protection, and so the Newtown Township police department became the next target of his financial generosity. He pumped millions into the department, outfitting each and every officer with the best body armor developed by the family company. He offered the use of his helicopter any time they needed it and built a shooting range on his estate where officers could train. He even allowed some members of the force to live on the estate grounds.

The condition was the same as when he was donating to the pentathlon team—he wanted acceptance. If the Newton Square police were going to take his money, they were going to treat him like one of them. In spite of the Newtown police's firm claims that John's money didn't buy him any special treatment, they did give him a badge to carry and a siren and radio for his car. To them, he may have been only an honorary cop, but as far as John was concerned, he was the real thing.

As Jean Liseter du Pont grew older and more infirm, John began establishing himself as a stronger presence on the farm, which made life interesting for the servants. Jean was demanding to be sure, but she was steadfast and predictable. John, on the other hand, had moods that altered wildly day to day, and some of his requests were downright odd. Plus, he had the annoying habit of cornering the farmhands and visitors to the estate and talking to them for hours about birds, seashells, and the minutiae of managing the estate. These conversations were always one-sided and tedious at best. At worst, they were disturbing.

He was always finding new things to do with his money, too. In 1980, while bidding anonymously, he paid $935,000 for the holy grail of stamp collecting, the British Guiana 1856 1 cent, black on magenta. At the time, the stamp was thought to be one of a kind. Owning it placed him among the greatest philatelists in the world, and added another title to his ever-growing list of accomplishments.

John's ego was growing to proportions that rivaled the size of his bank account. Some Haverford alumni came to him asking for a donation to the school so they could build a new science building, and John was more than happy to help. He wrote a check for one million dollars, but before handing it over, he told them his terms. He wanted his name on the building and it had to be so prominent that it could be seen from the street. He also wanted a teacher he didn't like fired and one that he did promoted. Haverford said no. John had never had his conditions refused before, and was so offended that he tore up the check in front of them.

John's strange behavior kept getting stranger, too. One Christmas day, Vicki Welch, who was living on the estate with her children and her husband Tim, a Newtown Square cop, looked outside her front door and saw a tank driving up to the house. She watched dumfounded as it came to a stop on the front lawn. The hatch opened, and John's head popped out, his face covered in blood and scratches.

"Can Tim come out to play?" he asked.

Mrs. Welch stared at him, speechless for a moment, and then replied, "No."

It wasn't long after that when John found a fox den near the Welch's house. Foxes were common on the estate grounds. Hunting them had been a great passion of both his parents. His father had even named Liseter Farm's horse stables "Foxcatcher." The den near the Welch's house was home to a mother fox that had just given birth to a litter of kits. John decided it would be funny to fill the hole with dynamite and blow it up, mother, cubs and all. Vicki, Tim and their children failed to see the humor, however, and took that incident as their cue to move off the farm.

Chapter 5: Love In the Second Act

In 1982, John broke his hand in a car accident and had to endure a series of orthopedic surgeries. It was a hard and painful time of his life, but it was also how he met twenty-nine-year-old Gale Wenk, an occupational therapist who would become his wife a year later.

Jean never approved of Gale. As much as she wanted to see her son wedded, the idea of him marrying beneath his class was an affront to her upbringing and the way she had raised John. Wealth married wealth; it didn't marry middle-class. But Gale's lack of status was what John loved most about her.

The wedding was a lavish ceremony and afterwards, the happy couple traveled the world together. When they returned to Liseter Farm, John moved out of the mansion and into a house he had built just for them on the estate grounds.

Now that the honeymoon was over, it was time for John to be completely honest with his new bride. So he sat her down and told her about the plot to kidnap him. Now that she was his wife, she would be a target, too. He told her she would have to be careful and vigilant to any and all signs of danger and if she saw something, she should report to him immediately. From now on, she would have to tell him whenever she went out and exactly where she was going and she was never, ever to go to the same place at the same time on the same day of the week. She couldn't be predictable. Being predictable made it easy for his enemies. She had to stay smart to stay safe.

When they had been dating, Gale had seen that John was more than a little odd, but this was a completely different level. She had no idea he was so delusional. She had no idea he drank so much, either. Sure, she had known he was a hard drinker, but since they were married, it seemed like he was getting drunk every single night. Sometimes he would even go days at a time without sobering up.

As the months passed, Gale kept thinking she had seen the worst in John, and he kept proving her wrong. It seemed as if he resented her for some reason he wouldn't explain, and sometimes that resentment was expressed in the form of violence. One night, after coming home from his aunt's funeral, he drunkenly stumbled into their bedroom and ordered Gale to help him get undressed. She came over and started unbuttoning his shirt and for no apparent reason, John punched her. She went down and he collapsed on top of her, gripping her by the throat and squeezing. As she clawed at him and gasped for air, he told her he was going to kill her. He was going to kill her and dump her body in the swamp. No one would ever find her, and even if someone did, it wouldn't matter. He controlled the police. He controlled everything. He had the money to make all his problems go away, and that included her.

But he didn't kill Gale that night, and she didn't leave him, either. She didn't leave him any time over the next five months when he tried to throw her in a fireplace, came after her with a knife and tried to shove her out of a moving car. But one night in February of 1984, Gale found the limit of what she was willing to endure for a life of luxury. She was getting ready for bed when John walked in and turned the TV to a channel that was playing "patriotic music," probably the National Anthem, which some stations would play just before they went off the air back in the days before 24-hour broadcasts. He turned the volume all the way up and Gale made the mistake of asking him to turn it down.

John turned to her. Why would she ask him to turn down the National Anthem? No true American would ever ask such a thing. Maybe she wasn't who she claimed to be. Maybe she was with the communists and a part of the plan to kidnap him.

John opened the dresser drawer and pulled out a pistol.

"You know what they do with Russian spies?" he asked, putting the barrel of the gun to her temple. "They shoot them."

Gale closed her eyes and cursed herself. She had seen bright flashing neon signs that something wasn't right with John, but she had stayed with him and hoped for the best. Now, it was too late. She was going to die for her mistake.

But John didn't shoot. He removed the gun from her head, then lied down on the bed and went to sleep.

One month later, Gale moved out and John filed for divorce. She sued him for abuse, but of course the case was settled out of court.

Chapter 6: John Du Pont – Wrestling Coach

John's forties had brought a rebellious streak with them, and he continued fighting against what he believed was expected of him. In 1986, he donated millions to Villanova University, which they used to build a basketball arena called (what else?) the Du Pont Pavilion. In exchange, he wanted Villanova to start a wrestling program, and in spite of the fact that the only previous experience he had with the sport dated back to his freshman year in high school, he wanted to be named head coach.

Wrestling had always been one of his great loves, but he'd been discouraged from pursuing it. Wrestling was barbaric and uncivilized. If a du Pont was going to be an athlete, it was supposed to be at a "country club sport." But at this point in his life, John could see that his destiny had always been tied to wrestling. Every other obsession he had ever had was just a substitute for it, and from here on out, he was only going to do what he wanted to do in life. He didn't care what his mother or anyone else thought.

Villanova agreed to his terms. John had what he wanted, but what he didn't have was the knowledge to make his brand new team thrive. As he'd learned during his expeditions with Tucker Abbott, when you lack something, you hire someone who has it, and you hire the best. So John set out to find the best wrestlers in the world to join his staff as assistant coaches. Among the first to join up was Mark Schultz, Dave's younger brother.

Like Dave, Mark had won gold in his weight class in '84. In fact, they were the first American brothers ever to win gold in the same Olympics. The Schultz boys were known for their incredible skill as well as their incredible ruthlessness in competition; Mark was almost disqualified from the games for excessive brutality when he broke his opponent's elbow. The Schultz boys fought to win and they fought hard, and that was exactly what John du Pont was looking for.

John also hired another champion, Andre Metzger, who was winning big on the World Championship circuit and was a solid contender for the '88 Olympics. According to Metzger, he received a yearly salary of $75,000 and a house on Liseter Farm. Not bad for an assistant wrestling coach of an unranked college team.

During John's reign at Villanova, he showed little to no regard for NCAA rules and regulations. He recruited new team members with the implied promise of payment, he allowed his wrestlers to stay at his estate, he flew them around in his Learjet and his helicopter, and he even bought them alcohol. Sometimes, he even showed up to practice drunk. His drinking had only gotten worse over the years, and now, it was really starting to get him into trouble.

"I hit a guy in my car and I think I killed him," John told Dan Chaid, another one of Villanova's overqualified assistant coaches, one night in December 1987. He was so drunk that he could have imagined the whole thing, and that was what Dan was hoping, but it wasn't the case. John had been on his way home from campus when he struck Lonnie Harris, a construction flagman, with his car. John stopped, saw the man lying there in the road, then drove away, telling witnesses he had a plane to catch. Fortunately, Harris survived, which was excellent news because it meant he could be bought. In the end, John was forced to pay a fine of $42.50 for leaving the scene of the accident. Any further police action would have required a complaint from Harris, but for some strange reason, none was ever filed.

Another night, after returning to the estate from a late wrestling meet, bad weather forced Metzger to stay the night in the mansion. John got drunk, same as he always did, but then something else happened. Something John had never done before.

He began coming on to Metzger. At first it was only unpleasant and awkward, like a joke that had gone too far and hadn't been all that funny to begin with. But John's advances grew in intensity. He begged Metzger to leave his wife and move into the mansion to be with him. When he refused, John dropped to his knees and clung to him, clawing at his body. Metzger retreated into one of the guest rooms, locked the door and waited out one of the longest nights in his life.

Metzger left the team and filed a lawsuit against John. For the most part, John left the handling of these matter to the lawyers, who settled the case out of court just as they always did. John denied any and all accusations of homosexuality, although he did offer to wrestle Metzger for the money he was seeking. Metzger opted for the check.

In 1988, after just two seasons, Villanova dropped its wrestling program. The administration's official position was that there was too little interest in the team to justify its existence, but the truth was that du Pont's antics had become too much trouble. If they allowed him to continue coaching with all the rules and regulations he was violating and the negative attention he was attracting, they would put their other sports programs at risk. So John found himself out of a job.

Sometimes, Olympic years were lucky for John, but that was not proving to be the case in 1988. He had already dealt with an embarrassing lawsuit and the collapse of his wrestling program, but it was in August of that year when he received the biggest blow of all — the death of his mother.

When Jean Liseter du Pont died, John was devastated. His mother had been there for him his entire life. She had been his best friend and constant companion. Without her, he was truly alone. His anchor to the world had been cut and now he was adrift.

Chapter 7: Foxcatcher

With his mother gone, John decided to do what she had done before him. When Dirty Willie left the family back in 1941, Jean had transformed the estate into a place of her own. Now it was John's turn. The first thing he did was fire almost the entire stable crew. With not enough manpower to go around, most of his mother's beloved ponies were put out to pasture. It was regrettable, but necessary. The estate wasn't going to be a horse farm anymore. John decided he was going to turn it into the most elite wrestling club in the world. He would build a state-of-the-art training facility and invite the best of the best to train and coach there. With a clear vision, he assumed stewardship of the estate and changed its name. Liseter Farm had been his mother's farm. His would be called Foxcatcher.

He spent over $600,000 turning his dream into a reality, but when he built it…they came. In 1989, the best wrestlers in the country began leaving clubs they had belonged to for years to join du Pont's Team Foxcatcher. One of the first to arrive was Dave Schultz.

Dave was one of the most respected names in amateur wrestling and a huge get for John's organization. In a lot of ways, John saw him as sort of a soul mate because Dave was one of the few people who really understood the depths of his isolation and loneliness. He had grown up being teased because of his looks and his dyslexia, but instead of sheltering himself from the world as John had done, he went out and met it head on. John admired his courage as much as he admired Dave's strength, strategic mind and god-given talent. And like John, Dave was constantly challenging himself, trying to become the best he could possibly be. And the admiration and affection wasn't one-sided, either. Dave saw himself in John. Wrestling had been Dave's salvation, and he understood what John was looking for in the sport. He wanted to help John, and he honestly seemed to think that he could.

But not everyone had as much patience with du Pont as Dave had. It wasn't long before his own little brother Mark couldn't stand being around John any longer. Living in luxury and training with the best athletes in the world had been a dream come true, and at times it was a lot of fun. John was always happy to share his booze and cocaine, and for a while, Mark had been happy to accept. But over the years, Mark had become convinced that John was a toxic presence. It wasn't just about what had happened with Metzger. It wasn't just about the drink and the drugs. It was all those things, but it was so much more. He just had a way of bringing you down. Mark always thought of himself as a happy guy, but lately, he always seemed to feel depressed. John had taken the fun out of wrestling. Mark decided that if he wasn't committed to the sport, he wasn't doing himself or anyone else any good. So he retired.

In 1990, John's cocaine use had become too much for Dan Chaid, too. He took John aside and told him he was going to help him get clean. At first, John tried to deny that he had a problem, but eventually, he broke down and started crying. He begged Chaid not to tell anyone. If his family found out he was a cokehead, they would take Foxcatcher away from him. And then he would have nothing.

Chapter 8: Unraveling

There was someone in the walls. John was sure of it. Somehow, his enemies had found a way inside the house. They were watching his every move, documenting his every word. One night, when he was sleeping, they would jump out and kill him. It was just a matter of time.

He had told Dan Chaid about it, and he had smiled and nodded, but John could tell he didn't really believe him. Maybe Chaid was in on it. Maybe he had been the one who helped his enemies get so close. He would have to do something about that.

In 1993, John met Patrick Goodale when he hired Aegis Security to help him search the estate for the people in his walls and the tunnels they were surely using to get on and off the property. Goodale was more than happy to oblige him. He spared no expense on his exhaustive search, ultimately charging John more than $200,000 for his services. They found nothing.

Still, John kept hiring Aegis time and time again. Goodale seemed to treat John's concerns as valid, which was more than he could say about his so-called friends. No matter what requests John made, whether he wanted Aegis to x-ray the ground under his driveway or install razor wire in the attic and inside the walls, Goodale took his requests very seriously.

John was slipping away. Every day his behavior became more erratic. Every day, he had another ridiculous concern or episode. One day he drove his car into a pond on the property, almost drowning his passenger. Another day, he demanded that all the treadmills be removed from the gym because he was afraid that they were taking him back in time.

Except for Goodale, the only person he could trust was Dave Schultz. Dave was his protector. But then again, Dave was always telling him that his many fears were unfounded. He told John that the trees weren't moving outside his windows. There were no ghosts coming out of the walls. The geese on the pond weren't casting spells on him. But none of that was true. Either Dave was wrong or he was lying. He couldn't be a part of the conspiracy, though. Not Dave.

That summer of 1995, John attended the World Wrestling Championship to support his team. He wore an orange jumpsuit and refused to speak to anyone who didn't address him as the Dalai Lama.

That fall, John's antics became less and less amusing. At one point, he told all the African-American wrestlers who were training at his facility to leave, declaring that Foxcatcher had become a KKK organization. John had decided that he couldn't have anyone or anything on the farm that was black. Black was the color of death.

On October 12th, 1995, Dan Chaid was lifting weights when John walked right up to him, pointed a machine gun at his chest and said, "Don't fuck with me. I want you off this farm." Chaid knew better than to argue with an automatic weapon, so he did as he was told, then went to the Newton Square police. They didn't take him seriously. That was just John being John. They wouldn't even let him register a formal complaint.

Lt. Lee Hunter did drop by the property to speak with John, though. The du Pont family lawyer had asked him to, and after everything John had done for the Newtown police force, Hunter was happy to oblige. When he arrived at the property, John told Hunter everything. He told him that one of the Team Foxcatcher wrestlers had attacked him in his sleep. He wasn't positive who it was, but he had his suspicions. He told him all about the conspiracy to ruin his name. He told him about the Russian spies that were about to invade Newtown Square in their bid to take over America. He told him that he was the Holy Child. Hunter reported back the details of the bizarre and unsettling conversation, but no action was taken.

Late in 1995, USA Wrestling's athletes' advisory council met to consider ending the sport's relationship with du Pont. It was a heated debate with strong arguments from both sides. Kenny Monday, who won the gold in the Seoul Olympics in 1988 and the silver in Barcelona in 1992, was begging them to sever all ties with du Pont. Monday insisted that John was crazy and if they didn't get away from him, something terrible was going to happen. In the end, thanks in great part to Dave Schultz's defense of John, it was decided that there would be no change in the relationship. After all, du Pont had just given them a $400,000 donation.

In November, Chaid returned to Foxcatcher Farm to pick up a van he had left behind. Before he departed for good, he stopped by the Schultzes' house and begged Dave to leave with him. Kenny Monday had been right. Du Pont was dangerous. Chaid had seen the writing on the wall in the form of a machine gun pointed at his chest. But Dave refused to leave.

It wasn't long after Dan had left when John showed up at Dave's house. He was drunk, reeking of alcohol. He had known Dan had been there. As a matter of fact, he was convinced that Dan was *still* there, and that Dave was hiding him. Dan was a part of the conspiracy, that's why John had kicked him off the team. And now, Dave was protecting him. Dave had become a traitor. As John ran through the house searching for Chaid, he tripped, fell and hit his head, cutting it. Dave picked him up off the floor and took him home.

John had done so much for Dave. He had given him and his family a place to live. He had provided him with everything he needed to make his comeback and maybe win a second gold medal. Besides, in some ways, Dave felt as if he was the only thing holding John together. Who knows what John would turn into if Dave abandoned him?

Two months later, Dave Schultz was dead.

Chapter 9: The Standoff

The family fortune was built on gunpowder. That was important to remember.

It had been two days since John had shot Dave Schultz dead in his driveway. Two days since John had barricaded himself inside the library of his mansion, which had been reinforced as a bomb shelter. He had plenty of food and water in there. He could wait them out for weeks, maybe months if he wanted to.

Seventy officers had surrounded the estate. Thirty or so were SWAT from neighboring districts, like team leader Andy Trautmann from Springfield, but most of them were from the Newtown Police Department. They had trained on that very property. They were wearing body armor John had supplied them with. And because of those things, they had done nothing when John threatened to kill his wife. They had done nothing after the hit-and-run in 1987. They had done nothing when he spewed all that craziness at Lee Hunter about Russian spies and the Holy Child. They had done nothing when he ran Dan Chaid off the grounds at gunpoint. Dave Schultz had paid for that with his life, and they were all paying for it now.

There was no telling what he could be up to in that house. The family fortune was built on gunpowder, after all. He could have a whole arsenal in there with him. What if he just decided to shoot them all to shit with his 50-caliber machine gun? Or maybe he was just going to blow up the whole damn house as easily as he blew up that fox den he found years ago. Apparently, he was crazy enough to do it.

The phone lines at Foxcatcher Farm had been damaged in a recent fire, so du Pont had been supplied with a cell phone so he could speak to the negotiators. He spoke to them often, but it was mostly just ranting for them to get off his "holy ground." He was also talking to his lawyers a lot, trying to make this whole thing go away. He didn't understand why his money wasn't enough to put an end to this as it had done every time he had been in trouble before.

It was Sunday, and it was bitter cold, even for late January in Pennsylvania, and now that it was starting to get dark, the chill was getting even deeper. They had shut down the mansion's boilers, so du Pont wasn't getting any heat. It had to be freezing inside the mansion by now. The negotiators raised him on the phone and when he complained about the cold, they offered to try and fix the boilers. But John didn't trust them. He told them he'd fix them himself, then hung up.

It was one of the snipers who saw him first. John had come out one of the mansion's rear doors and was heading towards the garden house where the boilers were kept. He appeared to be unarmed. Trautmann's unit was closest to the position, so they moved in.

"Police! Don't move!" Trautmann shouted.

John did as he was told, stopping in his tracks and putting his hands in the air...then turned and bolted back towards the mansion.

"Police! Stop! Don't move!"

Again, John stopped, putting his hands in the air. He turned to face Trautmann and saw six men with guns beginning to surround him. It had finally happened. His enemies had come for him, just like he always knew they would. He made another break for his house, and then felt his body fold under the impact of half a dozen armored SWAT members.

After fifty long hours, the siege was finally over. They had their suspect in custody and they didn't have to fire a single shot.

Chapter 10: In Custody

On February 9th, 1996 at a preliminary hearing, Judge David Videon read the charges against John du Pont and then asked him if he understood them. Sitting there in his blue hooded Team Foxcatcher sweatshirt, he leaned over to his lawyer, Richard A. Sprague and whispered something. Sprague nodded, then told the court that no, John did not understand. Still, the hearing proceeded.

The prosecutors called their only witness. A packed courtroom listened as Nancy Schultz recounted what she had witnessed two weeks ago, the day her husband died in her arms. When Sprague cross-examined her, he asked her a series of bizarre questions, such as whether she knew she was living on the holy land of the Dalai Lama and if she was aware if her husband had owned a bazooka. The prosecution objected to these questions, but they didn't need to be answered, anyway. What Sprague was doing was laying the groundwork for the insanity defense.

After the hearing, it was determined that John du Pont would have to stand trial for murder in the first degree, but first, he needed to be evaluated to determine if he was mentally competent to do so. Over the next few months, John was largely uncooperative with the psychiatrists and psychologists who tried to speak to him. And while he resisted assessment, his health began to decline. His lawyers asked for bail, but due to the two-day standoff before his arrest and the fact that he had repeatedly demanded his passport be returned to him, that request was denied.

Finally, on May 30th, du Pont's lawyer entered a plea of not guilty. While he was waiting for his day in court, he started managing his estate from his prison cell. One of his orders was that every building on the estate be painted solid black.

The color of death.

The 1996 Olympics

In a way, Dave Schultz did make it to Atlanta in '96.

"I know Dave is with me," Kurt Angle said. "I can feel him and it gives me strength." Then he went out and won the gold.

Nancy Schultz was also there, with her children Alexander and Danielle. After the murder, most of the Team Foxcatcher wrestlers, including Angle, deserted du Pont's facilities and were left with nowhere to continue their training. There was no way that Dave would have wanted his death to hurt any of his friends and teammates' Olympic chances, so Nancy started the Dave Schultz Wrestling Club and raised the money they needed to keep them training.

Some wrestlers, like Tom Brands, who won gold in the 136-pound weight class, stayed at Foxcatcher and even continued accepting du Pont's money. Brands tried to minimize the issue in interviews, but the other wrestlers ostracized him. These Olympic games were being fought in honor of Dave Schultz, and Brands was considered a traitor to his memory. But Brands was in the minority. During the games, Nancy embraced wrestlers from all over the world, crying and sharing memories of her husband with them. It was an environment that was full of love and healing. The Olympic games helped Nancy say goodbye to her husband. Now, all she had to do was make sure his killer was brought to justice.

Chapter 11: The Insanity Defense

They were asking him questions again, and videotaping him. There were two shrinks in the room, which meant he had twice as many people to distrust. His lawyer, Sprague, had said these men were here to help him, but Sprague was conspiring against him with the CIA. That's why he fired him.

They had no right treating him like this. Didn't they know who he was? He was the Dalai Lama, and he deserved diplomatic immunity. He was Jesus Christ. He was the last czar of Russia. He was the true successor to the Third Reich.

They kept asking about Dave Schultz, his protector. They said Dave was dead and that he had killed him. But he hadn't done that. Why did they think he had? Of course…the government must have sent a clone of him to do it. That was so smart. They could silence Schultz and convince the world that he was crazy at the same time. It was a brilliant plan. The Republicans must have been the ones behind it. They wanted his money and he wouldn't give it to him. That's why all this was happening. But it would be okay. Bill Clinton would help him.

*   *   *

After du Pont's videotaped interview was shown in court, one of the two psychiatrists, Dr. Phillip Resnick, testified that John was suffering from paranoid schizophrenia. Other experts agreed and on September 24th, Judge Jenkins declared that he was incompetent to stand trial. John was taken to a psychiatric hospital and returned to court two months later, on December 9th. He had been responding positively to treatment and was found competent enough to stand trial. A date was set for January 21st, 1997, five days short of the one-year anniversary of Dave's murder.

Du Pont's new lawyer, Thomas Bergstrom, chose to follow his predecessor's strategy and go with the insanity defense. It was a risky move, because it put the burden of proof on the defense rather than on the prosecution. As part of his plea, du Pont would be conceding the fact that he had killed Dave Schultz, and Bergstrom had to convince the jury that John didn't know it was wrong when he did it.

When the trial began, the defense argued that John was delusional and believed that Dave Schultz was part of a conspiracy to kill him. Assistant D.A. Joseph McGettigan claimed that du Pont was a master manipulator trying to get away with murder.

After three weeks of testimony and a week of deliberations, the jury decided that du Pont was guilty of third degree murder but mentally ill, which meant sentencing fell to Judge Patricia Jenkins.

Both the state and Nancy Schultz asked the court for the maximum 40-year sentence. Nancy wanted to be able to honestly tell her children that John du Pont would never be able to hurt them again. On May 13th, Judge Jenkins sentenced du Pont to 13 to 30 years in prison.

There were appeals, but the Supreme Court upheld the verdict. John lived out his sentence quietly and uneventfully, becoming eligible for parole in 2009. It was denied.

*   *   *

On Thursday, December 9th, 2010, at the age of 72, the bizarre life of John Eleuthère du Pont came to a quiet end. He was found unresponsive in his bed at Laurel Highlands State Prison and taken to Somerset Community Hospital where he was pronounced dead at 6:55 a.m.

Even after his death, he continued to surprise and amaze everyone who knew him. His will bequeathed 80% of his estate to Valentin Yordanov, a Bulgarian wrestler.

*   *   *

John Eleuthère du Pont was many things over the course of his life. He was a collector. He was a swimmer. He was a pentathlete, a scientist, a police officer and a wrestler. He was a philanthropist who gave generously to the causes he believed in. He was a teacher, a student and a coach. He was a son who loved his mother dearly and he was a true and loyal friend. He was also a murderer and a paranoid schizophrenic.

John's wealth enabled him to buy anything he wanted. It enabled him to set his own rules and vanquish his problems. It also kept him sheltered from everything, including the help he so desperately needed.

About the Author

Tim Huddleston was born and raised in Atlanta, Georgia and currently lives and works in Los Angeles, California. His proudest accomplishments to date include writing two-thirds of the ABC Family mini-series Fallen, and receiving a fist-bump from Catherine Keener during a game of Celebrity.

References

http://en.wikipedia.org/wiki/John_Eleuth%C3
%A8re_du_Pont

http://www.nytimes.com/2010/12/10/sports/
olympics/10dupont.html?src=twrhp&_r=0

http://murderpedia.org/male.D/d/dupont-
john.htm

http://www.rotten.com/library/bio/black-
sheep/john-du-pont/

http://abclocal.go.com/wpvi/story?section=ne
ws/local&id=7834281

http://topics.nytimes.com/topics/reference/ti
mestopics/people/d/john_e_du_pont/index.ht
ml

http://www.thedailybeast.com/newsweek/1996/02/04/an-eccentric-heir-s-wrestle-with-death.html

http://www.washingtonpost.com/wp-srv/local/longterm/aron/dupont022697.htm

http://www.nytimes.com/1996/01/27/us/dupont-accused-of-a-killing-holds-off-police-at-his-home.html?ref=johnedupont

http://intermatwrestle.com/articles/832/The-Life-and-Legacy-Dave-Schultz-Chapter-1-The-Day-Wrestling-Died

http://www.nytimes.com/1996/01/28/us/dream-of-wrestling-glory-is-cut-short-by-gunfire.html?ref=johnedupont

http://voices.yahoo.com/lunatic-sports-enthusiast-murderer-john-e-du-pont-7876196.html?cat=17

http://www.nytimes.com/specials/olympics/cntdown/0129oly-wre-dupont-shooting.html

http://www.nytimes.com/1996/02/04/sports/
sports-of-the-times-free-lunch-has-a-price-for-
athletes.html?ref=johnedupont

http://en.wikipedia.org/wiki/William_duPont,
_Jr.

http://en.wikipedia.org/wiki/Du_Pont_family

http://www.hagley.lib.de.us/library/collection
s/manuscripts/findingaids/will_dupont_sr_acc
2317.pdf

http://www.haverford.org/

http://en.wikipedia.org/wiki/Delaware_Muse
um_of_Natural_History

http://en.wikipedia.org/wiki/Dave_Schultz_(
wrestling)

http://www.raynesmccarty.com/newsevents/9
2-philadelphia-inquirer/176-schultzs-wife-
settles-claim-with-du-pont-.html

http://www.crimerack.com/2012/04/murder-of-david-schultz-case-file/

http://www.nytimes.com/1996/01/29/us/stepping-out-of-a-frigid-house-du-pont-heir-is-seized-by-police.html?ref=davidschultz

http://articles.philly.com/1997-01-29/news/25560167_1_david-schultz-thomas-bergstrom-pont-s-foxcatcher

http://articles.philly.com/1998-01-24/news/25747924_1_john-du-olympic-wrestler-david-schultz-thomas-bergstrom

http://www.mainlinetoday.com/Main-Line-Today/February-2007/In-Memory-of-a-Murder/

http://en.wikipedia.org/wiki/Modern_pentathlon

http://www.trutv.com/library/crime/criminal_mind/psychology/insanity/10.html

http://articles.chicagotribune.com/1997-01-28/news/9701280059_1_nancy-schultz-pont-defense-attorney-thomas-bergstrom

http://articles.philly.com/1996-02-04/news/25656708_1_john-du-pont-murder-of-olympic-wrestler-john-eleuthere

http://sportsillustrated.cnn.com/vault/article/magazine/MAG1080219/index.htm#

http://sportsillustrated.cnn.com/vault/article/magazine/MAG1008538/index.htm

http://articles.latimes.com/1996-01-31/sports/sp-35663_1_john-e-du-pont

http://en.wikipedia.org/wiki/DuPont

http://www.britannica.com/EBchecked/topic/172546/du-Pont-Family

http://articles.philly.com/1996-01-27/news/25653305_1_john-du-pont-foxcatcher-eleuthere-irenee

http://www.cnn.com/resources/video.almanac
/1996/index.html

http://sportsillustrated.cnn.com/vault/article/
magazine/MAG1142653/index.htm

http://msn.foxsports.com/olympics/wrestling/
story/andre-metzger-52-us-olympic-trials-greco-
roman-wrestling-john-e-du-pont-dies-in-prison-
shot-at-dream-042012

http://articles.baltimoresun.com/1991-07-
28/sports/1991209116_1_john-du-pont-big-
collection

http://www.workers.org/2010/us/dupont_122
3/

http://articles.philly.com/1997-02-
08/news/25536215_1_du-pont-dan-chaid-
foxcatcher-farms

http://articles.philly.com/1997-05-
14/news/25563653_1_murder-of-olympic-
wrestler-du-pont-john-eleuthere

http://caselaw.findlaw.com/pa-superior-court/1348932.html

http://www.schizophrenia.com/newsletter/197/197dupont.html

http://articles.philly.com/1997-01-28/news/25558512_1_david-schultz-defense-attorney-thomas-bergstrom-pont-s-foxcatcher

http://en.wikipedia.org/wiki/Delaware_Museum_of_Natural_History

http://articles.mcall.com/1996-01-30/news/3080538_1_olympic-wrestler-pont-s-estate-du-pont

http://articles.philly.com/1997-03-13/news/25572380_1_john-e-du-du-pont-olympic-wrestler-dave-schultz

http://query.nytimes.com/mem/archive/pdf?res=F20D16FD3859167B93C4AB1789D85F458485F9

http://www.equiery.com/archives/fairhill%20history/fairhill%20history.html

http://articles.philly.com/1996-01-29/news/25652557_1_boiler-system-friday-night-du-pont-boiler-police/4

http://www.people.com/people/archive/article/0,,20102757,00.html

http://articles.philly.com/1996-02-13/news/25655605_1_du-pont-accident-delaware-county-prison

http://articles.philly.com/1996-01-29/news/25653391_1_foxcatcher-national-training-center-john-e-du-facility-du